# OUT HERE IN IT ALL

## Poetic Alchemy of Grief, Identity, and Belonging

Poetry and Photography
By Coral Poppy

"OUT HERE IN IT ALL
Poetic Alchemy of Grief, Identity, and Belonging"
is an orignal work by Coral Poppy

ISBN# 979-8-9940431-0-3

# Dedication

To all my friends,

Somehow we got lucky enough to know each other. I am thankful for your curiosity, presence, grace, wisdom, and love. Y'all have taught me something I couldn't have come to know without you. Cheers to life my beloveds!

Veiw from up high - Sierra Nevada, USA

# Preface

I left the Christian cult I grew up in and lost every friend I ever had. Exiled, homesick, and searching for meaning— I threw myself into the world and learned how to play.

Giving up everything I thought I knew, I chose to live vividly, with radical acceptance, taking each step with utmost trust in my own footing. I traveled across 5 continents to the highest mountains and the lowest deserts, to the precipice of existential awe and back down to the simple sacred ground. I made a sincere effort to listen deeply to everyone and every place I encountered. I read, meditated, took Earth medicine, made impossible choices, breathed, lied, truthed, loved, lost, grieved, danced, adventured, and wrote poetry. For the first time in my life I was free to experience my self-hood.

Piece by piece, I rebuilt my fundamental understanding of what it means to be here on Earth— a process that's taken a decade and even still, I remain curiously baffled at every turn.

This collection of poems and images reflects experiences and epiphanies that came to me on this long and winding path to existential belonging. It is my hope that in some way my writings and photographs bring you closer to home on your own journey.

# Contents

## Section 1: **ACTUALIZE**



## Section 2: **CIVILIZE**



## Section 3: **AGONIZE**

## Section 4: **ALCHEMIZE**



## Section 5: **HARMONIZE**

Cordillera Huayhuash, Peru

Highliner Shianne McMinn in the rising sun

Section 1

# ACTUALIZE

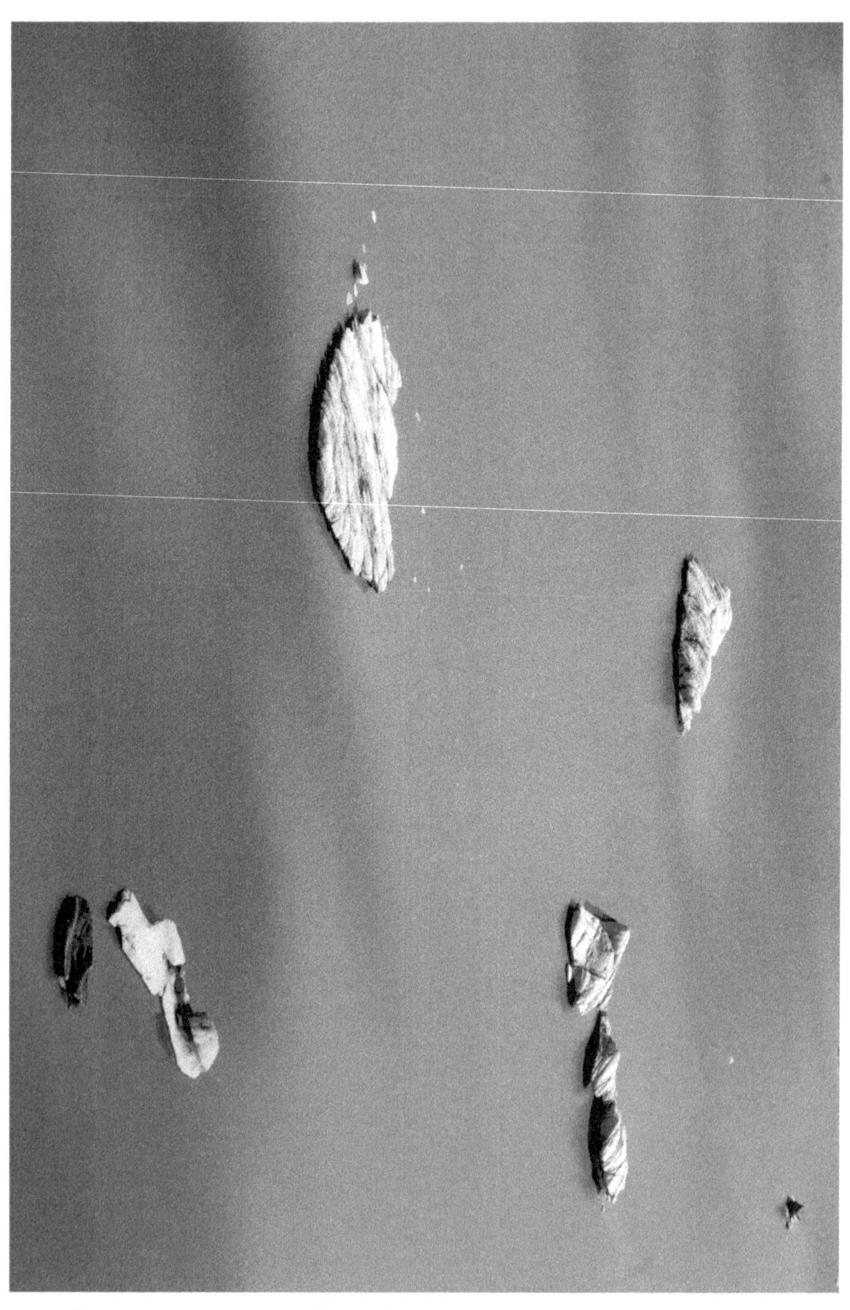

Ice cubes in cosmic soup - Fláajökull, Iceland

# WORDSCAPE

I smith words—
simply, to say,
privately, to pray,
lovingly, to lay out my inner scape

Mountains of mentions
Rivers of rambling requests
Terrain talks in tandem
Symphonies of sound serenading
Me, myself, and I
We, you, and they

Each syllable a rock
Each phrase a peak
Echoes ringing through valleys of thought
Words are wind—
carrying whispers, shouts, and sighs,
gusts of feeling
through the ravines between my ribs

In stillness between breaths,
I find forests of forgiven folly
and lakes reflecting hopes unspoken
My sentences stepping stones
leading me across the vast expanse
of all ineffable things

I shape words—
naturally, to navigate,
truthfully, to translate,
masterfully, to mold the unseen into form—

Yet I know,
this languishing symbology I craft
will never reveal this living landscape

## BECOMING OF A LADY

I can still taste sweet naive curious presence
The moment raw and pure,
wide eyes wandered onto the scene of my own unfolding

....Confusion

The ghosts of folks and lovers,
whose voices echo in my head,
are nowhere to be seen;
their appearance on this stage of my becoming
was composed of fleeting expressions
only once held mutually

Now distance has morphed me by velocity
I am–
compressed and stressed
one of many moving parts comprising some,
long lost
recently forgotten
moment

The intensity
of my desperate search for identity
is down to it's coals
The tendrils of youthful longing
burned up in the atmosphere as I pulled my feet back down to Earth
Slowly but surely
I stitched my spirit back into this skin;
bruised, cut, scraped, and still shining
with a fresh face of hope and naive splendor

I refuse to grow old and bitter in the name of wisdom
I would rather fly and scrape both my knees
than creep slowly in the shadows of caution

## WISE WOMEN

I used to hope that someday someone would recognize me;
so that they might tell me who I am

I have felt so lost
What I have mistakenly identified with
has cost me alot
Nothing is as I have thought
All these personalities I have tried on
seem to be like sand or snow in the hand

So given the chance and right circumstance,
I sat at the feet of wise women replete with discernment
I inquired,
not looking for answers but hoping instead to be inspired,

"Purpose...
is it something given, granted, cultivated, found,
or simply lived?"

Wise Women spoke:
"To be human is not to race but rather
to gather and place attention—
LISTEN
What is in the space between?
Can it be heard? Can it be seen?

The goal is not ascension, ask yourself:
Can I reach up and pull it down
to my root through my crown?
That is what **this** is all about
Find the route your light takes,
follow it true
Feel what is in your heart,
this is where we all must start"

## PLUCK THE DAY

Where light is cast
a shadow is drawn

I vomit love and hate
to find myself empty,
possessed by no spirit

Enchanting delirium,
once here I was entranced
Seduced by joy,
a hedonistic lush

But now putrid acid,
from the pit of my gut, reminds me,
what I am is not what I fill myself with

I thought if I collected joyous memories
I would have warmth in my pocket for dreary days
But.... Alas
Am I to be grateful for having had something to lose?

The day blooms with the dawn and wilts at dusk
Shall I pluck it?
The petals fall with or without

This is the life—
to walk, dance, run, and play
Here we are feasting
while the beasts rage elsewhere
*Carpe Diem*

## SEER

Visited by Vision in some space unseen
too far out to have simply been a dream:

I cried out to the Spirit of Sight,
"I am nauseous, dizzy, and sick from all this spinning!"
Then I was implored to sacrifice, not once but twice
I took both of my eyes from their sockets
they rolled like dice across a vast expanse
The Guardian then opened the cosmic door

The Spirit of Sight beckoned forth a swarm
Birds, bees, and butterflies proceed to peck and probe
through all my flesh to meet my bones
Some of my organs were spared,
saved to be prepared
The winged things lifted my lungs, heart, and liver
Levitating there in glaring light,
my tissues were washed in white
Brain, bladder, and kidneys were soaked in silver
The rest of my body was eaten and then regurgitated
I do not know how long I waited
but eventually the birds, bees, and butterflies
did give me back my bones, organs, and eyes

Now here I am having been re-membered
having surrendered deceptive perception
I am small specks of dust, around which thoughts neatly condense
What's the dew point today?
Shall we bring this phenomena to an Earthly birth?
After all, isn't this why the people pray?
To manifest the musing of the mind?
Let us rather steep awhile in the hanging mist
Truly, truly, I say to you,
clouds transform and dissipate with or without rain
I am here to do much the same

## THE GREAT MYSTERY

I screamed until my breath rasped
I struggled to cling to any thread at all
I gasped

Clawing at the skin of my very own incarnation,
unable to grasp myself
I was falling, falling
away into emptiness

Above it all,
so very far below

From here I could see the dark of darkness
I looked into all suffering;
of flesh and mind

I saw that in pleasure there was pain
and in love also sorrow
Even for nourishment
there must have been hunger

What more is there?
Beyond this or that

The Great Mystery,
I see her at the table of creation, she is blind
to all sensations of flesh and mind

Light and Dark sit at her two sides
If she opened her eye to gaze upon either
there would be none in the world of wonder
For there is no one without the other

Dylan Poppe and his shadow

Life and all it's treasures are simple - Huaraz, Peru

# EACH MOMENT

I can not will as I try
to get into or out of my mind
They say make peace with what's inside
but I've got as many issues as tissues
and these wounds aren't superficial;
something's clogging up the interstitial
but I've got an intuition, a present tense 6th sense
everything's gonna work out fine
Ain't got nine, no, only this one
and it's better than quite alright

Still I can not, though try as I might,
quantify and rationalize these things inside my mind
Is there heaven outside my cerebellum?

I'm still learning that it's good to have a yearning
Feeling peaceful ain't the same as being numb
I, too, done do the humdrum ho hum

I won't miss this chance
breath and let go
rise up and dance

Simply thankful,
that's all I know

Manaslu Conservation Area, Mansiri Himal, Nepal

## ALL ALONG

Over and over
Counting steps, one to one-hundred
Up through the steep of the mountains
I packed home into a backpack,
strapping need to my hips
I trust my feet
can carry the weight
of what it means
to be me

Squirrel works daily,
gathering plush mosses and soft strands
fallen from my finger combed locks
I hope she is warm this winter
May we both have enough
and nothing more

I wade through gold flecked rivers
I wonder at the wandering way of water
I sleep under falling peaks whose rise is met by infinite skies

It was here
in a dream I dreamt
my greatest dream had long ago been dreamt
From way out here in it all
I see there is nowhere to go
— After all the paths chosen
and many mistaken turns taken
in the fog at dawn of my life
I've come all this way to find
I have been walking
in my own footsteps
all along

Hallgrimskirkja, Reykjavik, Iceland

Section 2

# CIVILIZE

Concert Organ at Hallgrimskirkja - Reykjavik, Iceland

## CURIOUS COSMOS

What is there to do but sow the seeds we want to reap
Even in this garden full of weeds,
can we tend and mend the soil?
Is this breath worth our toil?

I see earthworm and their talents are still fully employed
Earth is a medicine wheel here to heal all that is mortal
Honey bee is searching for a flowering portal
In Summer's sunshine potent pollen still sticks
Rain runs, drops drip, no part of Earth is willing to quit

Hope is not mustered in desperate strife
no, it is the ever enduring nature of living life
We are not born alone to die alone
to wear our own souls through to the bone
I am here to be with you as much as to be me
To play is to see
One thread, one love, one breath
spans the universe out onward from the deepest depth

When in fear we think perhaps the end is near
Stop and listen, really hear
the buzz of everything learning
cosmic yearning
stretch and grow in curious musing
all this atomic fusing
The heavens implore us to explore
creative genius in simple existence

Beyond instinctual physics of inertia and hot resistance
in still vast timeless wandering wonder
flows a current that pulls us into and under
the gravity of love holding us together
temporal tether to the
ephemeral eternal elemental ether

Another sunrise at Swayambhu Mahachaitya - Kathmandu, Nepal

## AGE OLD QUESTION

Some folks preach about a savior
to take responsibility for our collective behavior
Others screech about absurdity
and the intrinsic absence of meaning

I am sick of the lies
these mind games and tricks to cauterize
the gaping, jagged wound
cut by the pain we give to each other
Even with the best intentions, we compete
...for survival?
Yet, I can not see you as my rival

Achilles heel, and apples bitten by Eve
perfection ideal, some kind of fantastic wish
to be greater than this?

The ecstasy of the moment,
the energy of the breath,
the way life flows through

There is evil for sure,
but still the snake in the grass seems to be friend
Truly, I know no foe
Oh the wheel turns, round and round again
From where I am and where once I was
I can possibly see how one day there might I be

There is, however, a line we find
it is drawn where we sign in the name of....

In the name of whom?
Justice.
A forged signature, another pawn in the game,
for still we have not seen her grace or her hand

Oh Honey, the milk is sour in the promised land
intolerable, unacceptable, inhumane
imagine the unimaginable

Who pulls the trigger, is it some one
or some result
of a world wide society that refuses to take fault
Oppressive regression in the name of progressive improvement
For what? I ask you, for what?

We have found very efficient methods to burn souls alive
in this hell fire we call our home under heaven

We cut short our breaths
to press forward faster toward some impending disaster
We toil, we fight, however ignorant of our own inner plight
This suffering is friction created by our societal fiction
We all search for some truth yet
all of it, all of it
uncouth

The Aspens told me, "We're all one"- Utah, USA

## BRING THEM BREAD

Some people repeat what they are told—
and boldly so,
chest puffed up,
tones getting louder and louder
to be heard above some imagined other

And really, really,
I imagine they are speaking quietly,
eyes pleading,
earnestly searching for a nod of recognition
They just want their opinions to be important,
thoughts to be valuable,
your attention to be held in a place of honor

But oh, these proud boys, how they squander
the hard work they stand on
Many days slinging the weight—
the backbone of America is breaking
in the hot sweltering sun,
in an earth warming,
fields fallow,
locusts swarming

Hands tied, lips zipped, healthcare denied
We who protest this unrighteous greed
will be held in contrition—
if not first by bullets in the street,
then at court and the pious pulpit,

Grandma sits by Sister Jones in the pew
Phew—
they damn well fart in church too
But oh, they swear and the elders agree,
that in this congregation,
shit don't stink

Maybe someday we all might come to see
our own youth bleeding on the street,
for choices made on their own,
from a heart that ought to have been
worn on a sleeve—
but instead has been worn down,
crushed,
and ushered into hiding

When will all these folks realize
that it is us, the exiled ones,
who have minds,
who are curious in innocence

It is we who have thrown our pearls at the swine—
the politician and the preacher
both feature the mark of the beast
and have long lost the law of love
that Jesus, all the Women, Prophets, and Saints
died in the name of

The only lake of fire
is in the pants of liars
who stand in front of people who are meek
and rain down condemnation

But I'll tell you what:
Even Satan can speak of Heaven
and hold God's holy words
But never will Spirit
move mountains in the name of hate

So what instead
shall this nation do
with Spirit?

Can we hold it lightly,
grasp each other tightly,
dance with it—and live?

Can we forgive?

Naomi and Ruth—
Those ladies had nothing to prove
They lived quietly, simply,
but also spat at the ground of men
who tried to dictate a way of life
not suited, nor rooted, in faith
but rather in process and property

And what did God say?
Not even a sparrow may fall
without the attention of the divine heart
And if your hairs are numbered,
aren't also those
on the heads of people
who choose to cover theirs?

Jesus traveled to raise a young girl from the dead—
but those he so saved
still do not defend
children who are slaughtered in their own beds,
day and night,
in the name of some earthly fight
over land grabs and ideals

There's simply no Awe left in 'Merica
it's all gone berserka
under consecrated capitolist control,
tryanical exploitation of public perception,
all the sheep in a field of deception

How, oh how do we keep our heart whole?

First off, remember,
only crooks reach for justification in the holy book

People, people—
real peaceful people—
will look you in the eye,
and show up,
and listen,
and maybe cry when you cry

These institutions and corporations
are not even built on stone
No—
rather, they sit on paper
Paper that has never even been printed
GDP got one thing right:
Profit from the labor of our numbered days
is GROSS domestic product

A country in debt
does not owe cash—
but rather the exponential potential of it's people
The gears are turning in this machine,
and what is the output?

Well, the most profitable thing
that mankind can think of
has always been:
War

The Supreme Court is tripping
on the power they imagine
their gavel still yields
But this broke-ass generation cannot sit
We do not agree with their particular interpretation
of the Constitution—
that has long since been divorced
from its original form and purpose

We demand restitution
for our stolen bodies

No doubt
there's no marrow left in the bones
of those who laid down these laws
on forsaken dreams

Where are you bursting at the seam?
Is there an abundance somewhere inside of you?

And would you—
would you be willing to share
with those less aware
in the moment you stand in front of them?

Pull up the bucket from the well
and offer drops of clean water
It can be simple
So simple
Feed the people
Bring them bread
Bring them bread

Courage is going out into the world
and showing up with love—
day after day
in the trenches
Look around—
all these worn-out citizens
Violence and efficiency—
this is not the purpose
for which we are meant

We the People
We Dissent

## TAKE A BITE

Next day delivery dawned on the anthropocene
Packages arrive
Anything on my mind
is here in no time
No time
No time
Somehow I am losing all of mine
There is a pace I can not keep

When were we happy to just spin around the sun?

Gnashing teeth grinding down coffee stained enamel
Resilience replaced by popular demand
Though this greed is ravenous
salivation does not drip,
desire does not pool
So therefore, how are we to digest any morsel consumed?

Long ago the flavor of crumbs
met lips simply delighted to be touched
Oh to be tantalized in such a way

A remedy must *still* exist
We act astonished as if this is all so new
but back in the day they say Eve gobbled the fruit
meant to be savored for its heavenly flavor
The Earth does also dangle from some cosmic branch,
perhaps this Garden was meant to be nibbled

Go on, take a bite...
but not
quite
to the core

The melting edge - Fláajökull, Iceland

Section 3

# AGONIZE

## STRIVING

Why do I reach even when my arms are full?
Can I drop the weight of what I have without losing what I want?
Does the treasury decay if it is not constantly filled?
Does rust consume my excess as I claim abundance?
Is it that nothing is mine to keep?
Perhaps today only borrows,
for tomorrow brings what it may,
not as I will.

Thingvellir National Park, Iceland

## HIGH CONTRAST

I do not understand why
my heart is always full, so joyful and bright
yet always ripping apart
breaking under the weight of sorrow
suffering the constriction of time

My heart thumps against the limits of its form
Light of love, limitless and free
ought to burst forth from my chest leaving my flesh torn and shredded
Instead of this,
love merely oozes through the walls of the cells that contain me

A small drip from my lips in words of well wishes
I thought that maybe my finger tips could send a flood but no,
by the time it reaches you it is only a faint warmth,
soft heat from a single candle

I wish love could engulf the world
send it into flames, burn it as fiercely as it burns within me
There is no hiding from the pain love brings,
no escaping the agony it reveals

The deeper I love, the more I understand hate
The more I know joy, the more I feel the world's wounding
The closer I hold you, the further you will fall in grief
I do now know how I can be so full and yet still so empty

To be or not to be,
to numb the extremes or revel in this visceral ecstasy

# FERTILIZE

In my womb,
the primeval spell was cast
Second by second,
light unraveled in the dark
Nucleic acids alchemized the thread of life
according to the vestige of our ancestors

But what of it when the initiation does not complete?
This sacred ceremonial dance of hydrogen and nitrogen
will not conclude;
the drum of mitosis will cease

If I could have ran, I would have
And even though I tried to freeze,
like a statue of picturesque stone,
I continued to expand
I was a vessel that did not know it could be filled
This proliferation— a force beyond my will
Little electric pulses, all her own, thumped to the rhythm of life
I name her Passion—
derived from the perfect passive participle *passus*— "to suffer"
Passion, perfect passing particles of love

There are not ten toes, nor fingers, no little nose
And no one will know that Mother is me
These wrinkles and sunken eyes by my year twenty-five
is not all I have to show
Oh, how my heart has grown

My blood and hers, I poured on the soil at the root
where the honeysuckle meets the passion flower
Coagulated crimson offering
Gestated tissues decompose in my garden
Vines drink up nutrients I built in my womb
and surrendered so soon

Total solar eclipse - Oregon, USA

## ETERNAL

Mortality is the basis for creation,
decay refines elemental energy

Flowers fertile in summers heat
velvet petals, soft and supple
Even these will dry
in the very sun
that which brought their fruition forth

Fruit will fall and feed the life
that will live through this changing season

The land will take its rest
as the cold descends
Hush, hush

Eternal cosmic vibrance,
surrenders to the Gian womb —
again

## AN ODE TO PASSING

Your last breath leaving —

Snow soft mountains
Color kissed sky
Ocean beloved land

Earth inhales

Mother cradles, then sets free

Where the wind stopped - Iceland

## I STILL HOLD YOU

To know loss
is to hold a finite jewel
against infinity

Death is a black hole
Physical form falls beyond the event horizon
No glimmer of light leaps forth

From a singularity, they say, this all transpired
True, for once I wasn't alone when I had you
Condensed love makes life soup,
just add water

Love caught in time
is a life lived, perhaps well
or either more of a brawl
All of the beauty
grotesque as some of it may have been
is gobbled up all the same in the maw
of a stirring, swirling, mass of existence
The weight, the pressure
— something has to give

Does darkness swallow us whole when we go?
Or does light scatter, just at the surface;
In the very final moment, did you escape?

Everything is so present
I call to you, my beloved
you are so real to me, the love I have is so now
it can not be that belovedness has passed

And so forever more I search for my beloved;
in the fluttering of butterfly wings,
in symphonies at dusk
in the caw of a lone crow
in sunlight trickling through trees
in the dancing rustle of leaves
Ahh I glimpse you there,
in shimmering alpine lakes,
in the all the delights of day,
even in the loneliness of your absence, inside this quiet ache
These are the places I still hold you,
my beloved

Two souls, fated but free - Chitwan, Nepal

## GRIEF

All my hopes
known but unrealized
pour down like monsoon rain
in a desert that moments ago was so still and dry

Sky is falling —
This heaviness can not be held up
Waters of life demand to be welcomed back to dirt

Sand, solid but never once rooted, beneath my feet,
swept away like memories in the wind
Left adrift, unanchored, in the vast unknown
Nothing left of what could have been

I am now in a sea with no shore
I am the deserted island

My heart sinks beneath waves that crash, churn, and never find rest
Must I learn to breathe underwater,
to suck air from the deep?

Is this how it must always be?
All at once– or nothing at all?

 The Racetrack, Death Valley, Nevada, USA 

## AGAIN

By and by,
grief loosens from my sinew,
it creeps from my heart

I choose to let go
the comfort of holding it in
and the old familiar pain of losing myself in it

I run and scream
Stomp the dark back into the earth
I dance and dream
Reaching on out to community

In freshly turned soil,
life roots again
growth in the ache
blossoms in the light

And so it goes
to love and behold —
again

Passion Flower - medicinal flora, my front yard

## SELF-HEAL

Longing for
what could have been
dissolves

The heart
no longer holds
what cut it

A thorn
is lifted from the side—
slowly,
without blame—
and returned
to the rose

Self-Heal - medicinal flora, Seekseekqua, Oregon, USA

## CHANGING WIND

What is whooshing around me?
I was still, peaceful,
nested

But there's a new front blowing in
The cozy dust blanketing my familiar place
is stirred

In my grandmother's pasture
Where the horses and I were raised
Where my training wheels came off
I was told to find my balance
I was told that if I have to stop
I better be ready to put my foot down

Hooves, wheels —
I discovered wings
Picking myself up and carrying on

I fluff my neglected feathers,
I ought to mozy
Though I feel great haste,
I am no defenseless chick,
this is only a changing wind

Freedom, how to be?

Self-portrait, Portal of Fire - Oregon, USA

## LIFT

I watched an eagle beat its wings
against a headwind, climbing upstream,
only to turn in the air and face
the same resistance again

And I wondered—
how does an eagle know
when to fight
and when to flow?

I, for one, do not know
When to hold on,
when to let go

How much heart to offer?
How much will to be willing?

Does the eagle sense a future written into wind,
or simply trust its wings
to answer what arrives?

One thing is certain:
fish learn the river by swimming it

Maybe knowing isn't conviction at all,
but a practiced attention—
a willingness to meet resistance
until it becomes lift

Manaslu Conservation Area, Mansiri Himal, Nepal

Richness of rot - Mycena in the Redwoods

Section 4

# ALCHEMIZE

## THE WAY OF WATER

Be like water,
take the path of least resistance
If we get stopped– rise up and flow over,
otherwise, go around, or in time, work through

Only go when pushed or drawn
otherwise be still and simply seep
down and then again up
Weave through root and branch,
from leaf, transpire back into it all

The whimsy of the water path
is not known until after
roaring rushing rapids
Toss us against rock and a hard place
turning, tumbling
We beg, "Under current, pull at us,
rip us from this chaos!"

Surrender

This is the way of water;
to flow into the unknown
to be transformed as we are drawn forward

Gurgling spring
from ancient rains,
long ago trapped in stone
Flowing, peaceful, bubbling brook
from melting mountain top,
soon to be a drop in the ocean

To shape and be shaped
— this is the purpose
Temporal forms in motion

 Thingvellir National Park, Iceland 

## PEACE

Every wish I have ever made,
on the breath of a blown out candle,
on the tail of a shooting star,
at the kerplop of a coin in a fountain,
by way of incense smoke at the altar –

Every wish, every prayer
has been made for peace
In my home, in my heart, in my world

Yet, I did not expect peace to arrive by way of acceptance
I let loose my grasp, unclenched my jaw,
"Okay, alright, if it must, so it is, let it be"

Cultivating inner peace... haa what a farce!
There's nothing to grow, no striving, or tending
Peace seems to be some kind of return
...surrender...

Yet, once I sense I have it
it's almost already gone –
soon as the thinking starts,
the experience stops

After all, is not bliss found in ignorance
Only the innocent fool discovers anything untainted by expectation

## SMALL MIRACLE

Fire fortifies life-force–
in passion, anger, rage, love, desire
What is it we're burning?

"Follow your heart,"
they say, as if mine could tell the difference
between true north and magnetic longing
Most days, it's just my feet that choose—
slow, steady, stubborn—
the next patch of earth to trust

I'm learning to offer the flames
everything too heavy to haul up this mountain
Fear, brittle certainties, resentment, the need to be good,
and the performance of bravery

Return to the small miracle:
Breath, step–breath, step

To go along living, doesn't require a firmly planted foot
When it comes down to earth,
I'm always surprised at how little traction
is necessary to keep on keeping on

## REVIVAL

Frolic to the forest
behold this season's chorus
Sit silently by the stream,
search for the unseen

From where does this cerulean torrent continuously flow?
Each Spring everything looks new,
what is old and where did it go?

The forest speaks, but not in words
Messages arrive on the wings of migrating birds
Listen... here;
fiddleheads sing of first harvest,
trilliums keep time in ephemeral color

Surviving sooty cedars stand proud
amongst the charcoal of their fallen comrades
Look out below!
Savory 'shrooms erupt from silty soil
Aha— what remains to be seen is often underfoot

pyriscence?
Oh yes!
Be left fresh and fertile
just as flame churned earth
Let the fires burn
strip away what is dank and dense
Great heat, necessary release
Let sweet rain soak through,
Life begins anew, yet never did it cease

## EAT FRUIT

Taste the sun
Golden light wrapped in sweet skin
Each bite carries the warmth of Summer
the glow of days passed remains contained in
sunshine sugar filled flesh

Sun sinks into soil, awakens the seeds
and rises again in forms—
oranges, peaches, plums, mangos, melons, figs, and berries

We delicately hold delectable brightness
and press it to our lips
Salitavate, suck, and slurp
Each bite is a memory of light
A burst of life that ripened under Summer's blushing sky

We consume the sun in slices,
in juices that run down our fingers
As shine tantalizes taste buds
our cells soak in sweetness

Eat the Earth's joy,
alchemized light
Summer's gold
Feel the sun alive inside— Eat fruit!

Wild Strawberry - Seekseekqua, Oregon, USA

## IN RICHNESS OF ROT

Microbes munch on molecules
Derangement from form
Free the elements!

*Moksha* through mush and slime
Oh God, what is that stench?
Sublime scent of off-gassing *samsara*

Does the nitrogen of dismembered leaves
remember when it was green;
Does it recall the taste of sunshine?
I think it must,
the double helix in each cell of mine
turns to the sun to be kissed as an expectant lover

Tectonic turmoil turned the soil
Minerals migrated and moved
Rearranged arrangement

This year an iron spirit, from an ancient mountain,
resurrected in my spinach
She once held the spine of a ridge
Now she flows in my blood,
blushing in my cheeks

Adorn the altar with marigolds
Harvest fruits, roots, and mushrooms
Carve the squash
Celebrate the richness
Let the rest rot

Tiny infinities, lichen on alder bark - Seekseekqua, Oregon, USA

Dylan Poppe harmonizing with sand bluffs - California, USA

Section 5

# HARMONIZE

## EARTHEN VESSEL

Plunge down into cold high waters of rapture
Gasp but do not breathe

Wrapped in sunlight shimmering silently,
soothing, soaking love into a hollow
It is here I find some golden chalice —
I am disturbed to find this bygone grail

I have been searching for it
Though I thought I might encounter it once again as some new relic
fresh, beautiful, shining
I thought to find it as I found it before,
naive, open, curious cup

But to see it here tarnished by tannins,
dank dried remnants of what once belonged

How painful it is to be empty once one knows the feeling of being full
I recall when this chalice once overflowed at a grand feast;
Where I chewed chutney with creamed curries
The chalice glowed as it was filled by The Goddess herself
I took several sips and bid thanks
But alas the table turned,
the chalice spilled
Whoopsie daisy the whole damn thing
Forsaken nectar
My eyes would not meet one of The Goddess's thousand
Ashamed to have taken the drink of love lightly

Not understanding the weight; the force of gravity
on something of such great matter
I thought perhaps The Goddess would never offer it up again,
would not pour that sweet sacred light for me

I have long learned to take the offering
in cupped hand
one lap at a time
Without vessel to hold —
I take all my blessings only at the spring
I often wish to take some for later
When I am scorched as cracked land thirsty

Perhaps I might learn to honor the present
like berries plumping only in season, only after

blossoms blush with pollen
brushed by delicate critters
rich in the grace of Summer's sweetest gold

Soil who houses The Roots spoke up,

"Haven't you been told, it is commonly know,
as an earthy form, you and the vessel are one
The Goddess, she will pour for you, honored guest,
darling lover, one worthy of warmth,
beholder of wonder, your heart full of splendor
You shall always be splendid,
put your cup out once more
for it is not meant to be stored nor hoarded

Stagnant waters are only abodes for the slippery and slimy beings
You, precious, porous, earthly one
hold nothing and always be full."

## BORN FREE

You were born dancing
Remember?

Before the world told you to sit still,
you were a whirling joy

God dropped rhythm in your blood
and called it love
The heart beats so that you might
spin to its drum

Dance until your thoughts dissolve—
until only breath and heat remain

Val Olson in flames

## FAR OUT

Do you ever get this far out feeling?
Zooooming, zooming,
zooming
out
Shrinking, shrinking,
shrinking
in
Falling, falling,
falling
away

Until...
you are so small and so large,
standing on the teeniest, tiniest tip,
a precipice

A little bit of paranoia creeps in
as you wonder if anybody else knows
That you are

—barely here at all
There's peculiar peace
as you notice that everything
everything, everything, everywhere
—is barely here at all

Delicate existence eloquently balanced
Life lives, heart beats, electrons elate in perfect energy exchange
No effort exerts upon all autonomic oscillating waves of wonder

BREATHE!

Just right here .

# MUSE

You tune a guitar
Suddenly the air sweetens

Your presence, our song
untangles the quiet spark
All thoughts turn to light

## FEAST

Come feast, my friends!
Full course, improvised menu
Let the complexities tantalize your palate;
savor this carnival of flavor:
notes of brightness and earthy depths
May our days go down the gullet fully chewed

You pluck the steel strings
We'll sing and tend the fire
Puff, puff, pass –
smoke curling, a lazy blessing
Love knows how to find us here

Love, a turmeric stained ladle
spooning nourishment into the bowls
of those knocking at an hour too late

Love, lazing about the morning
sipping steamy sumatra,
piecing puzzles patiently

Nowhere to go and nothing to do;
everything needed is gathered here—
or drifting near, like a friend arriving late

Come as you are,
stay longer than you think you should

By fate or some splendid serendipity
these moments were set in motion,
etched eons ago—
relish them now!

## TRUE LOVE

If you are going to love, you ought to love for love's sake
and not for want
And so a love lost is still love
within and without

Leave the world to be as it may
seek not to change a thing
and yet still,
bring love

Scrub love into the cracks
where it may mingle with grime
Cry love onto Summer's wilting flowers
Scream love into the wind when your belly burns with anger
Ask no one for your love back
Ask no one where their love is
Set all love free!

Heart puddle - Oregon, USA

## WHAT TO DO ABOUT IT ALL

A child wonders where the butterflies sleep
The world has many secrets it keeps,
and for so many reasons why is not mine to know

If you are full of oughtness,
if you really must go,

Go galumphing out into the world,
heart upon sleeve, spirit unfurled
A bona fide act of revolution,
the most courageous solution,
is to call upon grace,
not from some place far away and above
but found in a feindiously simple Earthly love

Flying friend on a strawberry leaf - Seekseekqua, Oregon, USA

## I'LL BE DARNED

Even my holey socks can be darned instead of damned

Pessimism stitches with a threadless needle
As if opinions ever shelter the flesh
As if the doers care what a critic has to say
from a throne of resigned doom

And surely I don't deny doom
It's just that I believe in all the things
between now and then

Courage is hands of the hopeful
unraveling the thread of possibilities
So that the world can be made—
woven, knit, sewn, mended

Spirit of Redwood Burl

## THE WEIGHT

In the morning when all things seem possible—

Prioritize pleasure
Generate gentleness
Dawdle down to the river bank
Sink your toes down into the mud
Wiggle and squish
This is **it**,
slow soggy dirt
and your giggle

Besides, what is all this heavy flesh for,
if not the sensations of the world?

Pair of Opposites - Warm Springs, Wasco, and Paiute Tribal Land

## MEET THE AUTHOR

Coral Poppy writes poems the way she moves through mountains– curiously, reverently, and with a willingness to go into the unknown. She is a backcountry-snowboarder, psychonaut, highliner, forager, and applied mycologist but most truly she is a person that lives vividly. She is shaped by the elements and unseen forces, and like all of us – carved by love and loss. Her inspiration comes from her experiences of peak flow states, where life flows along the thin line of now above a vast expanse- that dazzling feeling of looking down from high places, where the world spreads out in all directions and something ancient in the heart seems to settle and rise at the same time. With deep reverence, her poems celebrate the cycles of nature and her own wild mysteries - where fear becomes awe, where solitude becomes insight and where meaning blooms in the places we are most afraid to look.

Coral Poppy in her home range, Central Oregon Cascades

www.ingramcontent.com/pod-product-compliance
Ingram Content Group UK Ltd.
Pitfield, Milton Keynes, MK11 3LW, UK
UKHW062308290726
14090UKWH00018B/945